HAS SATAN TAKEN A SEAT IN YOUR HOUSE?

*Compelling Stories that Will Teach You
How to Keep the Enemy Out*

Ivory Johnson

KishKnows
PUBLISHING

"I know where you live—where Satan has his throne. Yet you remain true to my name. You did not renounce your faith in me, not even in the days of Antipas, my faithful witness, who was put to death in your city—where Satan lives."

(Revelation 2:13 NIV)

Has Satan Taken a Seat in Your House?

Compelling Stories that Will Teach You How to Keep the Enemy Out

by Ivory Johnson

Cover design, editing, book layout, and publishing services by KishKnows, Inc., Richton Park, Illinois, 708-252-DOIT

admin@kishknows.com
www.kishknows.com

ISBN 978-0-578-33054-9

LCCN 2021924740

Some Scripture references may be paraphrased versions or illustrative references of the author. Unless otherwise specified, all other references are from **King James Version of the Bible**.

Scriptures marked **NIV** are taken from **THE HOLY BIBLE, NEW INTERNATIONAL VERSION®, NIV®** Copyright © 1973, 1978, 1984, 2011 by Biblical, Inc.® Used by permission. All rights reserved worldwide.

DEDICATION

...*To **God**, who is the head of my life.*

...*To my husband of twenty-two years, **Pastor Howard**.*

...*To my parents, **Joe** and **Alberta**...thank you for your unconditional love. There are not enough words to describe how much I love and respect you.*

...*To my children, **Carnardo**, **Carl**, **Gabriel**, and **Ida**...you continue to amaze me with your accomplishments. I appreciate and use your faith and ambition as a stepping stool to indulging in faith.*

...*To **my grandchildren**...I thank you for the smiles and the joy you bring to me.*

"The Lord will rescue me from every evil attack and will bring me safely to his heavenly kingdom. To him be glory for ever and ever. Amen."
(2 Timothy 4:18 NIV)

TABLE OF CONTENTS

INTRODUCTION

The works of the devil are many. He causes…

Anger…*Hatred*…Deception…*Divorce*…
Depression…*Sickness*…
Lying…*Fornication*…Blasphemy…
Adultery…Fear…

*"'All this I will give you,' he said,
'if you will bow down and worship me.'
Jesus said to him, 'Away from me, Satan!
For it is written: Worship the Lord
your God and serve him only.'"*
(Matthew 4:9-10 NIV)

You are about to meet four very different people from very different walks of life. They have nothing in common except this: they are willing to take a stand, no matter the cost.

CORA AND FRANK

Chapter 1

*"It is better to take refuge in the Lord
than to trust in humans."*
(Psalm 118:8 NIV)

Cora sat quietly, staring out the window on a windy October day. She was thinking about the "instructions" that her husband had given her. She was never to leave their home without him, and she was not allowed to let anyone into their home if he was not there.

For years she had followed his instructions…but today she wanted to go to church. Surely he could not be upset about *church*!

As she was getting ready, fear washed over her, and she sat back down on the bed, thinking about what would happen if she disobeyed him. As she sat looking out the window, she watched the leaves swirl, listened to the wind hitting the side of the building and thought, "He left three days ago, and I haven't heard from him." She made up her mind, finished putting on her clothes, and found his "secret hiding place" in the back of the closet. She took fifteen dollars out of the box and called for a cab.

It had been years since Cora had been to church, and she was touched to see that everyone remembered her and was happy to see her. Pastor Robertson smiled when he saw her sitting in the pew. He recalled her lovely voice and asked her if she would bless them with a song. She sang *His Eye Is on the Sparrow*, and there was not a dry eye in the sanctuary.

Cora felt the Holy Spirit as she returned to her seat, praising God. She had not felt this good in a long time, and tears started to roll down her face. She felt someone touch her shoulder and turned to find her friend, Betty. She said, "Cora, we need to talk after church." Cora nodded and sat down.

After the service was over, Cora went to talk to Pastor Robertson. She asked him if he could call her husband and set up some counseling for them. He explained that he had tried to call but her husband had changed his number, and he hadn't been able to reach him. He said, "You can certainly ask him to call me, and I will gladly speak with him." He had been concerned about her for a long time because he knew that her husband was twenty years older than she was, and he knew her husband's past.

As she left the church, her friends asked her to come back and join the choir, exclaiming that they missed her so much. She said she would, but in her heart she knew he would not let her come back.

Outside, Betty was waiting to talk to her. Cora walked over and asked her how she was doing, and Betty said, "I have been wondering the same thing about you. Let's go to my car—it's too cold out here." As they walked, she asked Cora what happened to her car and she said, "My husband has it, and he's out of town."

Betty offered to drive Cora home, but she refused. She thanked her and said she would take a cab. "Why would you do that?" Betty asked. "It really isn't a problem. I will take you home." Cora said nervously, "That's okay. Frank will get upset if I am with someone other than him."

Betty said, "What are you talking about? What do you mean he gets upset if you are with someone else? Is he like that with you?"

Cora lowered her eyes and said quietly, "Yes. I took a chance coming today. I am praying that he is not there when I get home." She explained that she was afraid of him, but she couldn't leave because he would find her.

Betty wrote down her number and handed it to Cora. She told her to call if she ever needed anything and then she said gently, "You must love yourself first and then others will love you. You must stand up to him, and tell him that you won't take it anymore. You need to separate from him until he gets some counseling."

Betty took Cora's hand. She said, "I have enough money to take care of both of us. God has truly blessed me, and I'm well off. Please come and live with me. He won't know where you are, and you don't have to go back to him. He's not treating you right."

"Husbands, love your wives, just as Christ loved the church and gave himself up for her."
(Ephesians 5:25 NIV)

Cora said, "I need to go back. He is my husband, and as long as I do what he tells me to do, everything will be okay." Betty looked at her. "Cora! What has happened to you? You must know that a demon has enslaved you! That is not from God. No one has the right to take over someone else's life! This is not right! I am going to talk to Pastor Robertson about this to see how we can help."

Cora got out of the car. She thanked Betty and said, "I will think about it. Will you ask the church to put us on the prayer list? I love you, my friend." Betty had tears in her eyes. She nodded and said, "I love you more."

CHAPTER 2

As *the taxi grew close to her building*, Cora realized that her husband was home. She asked the taxi driver to stop a few doors down the street, then walked quickly to the side of the building where she stopped for a moment and said a quick prayer. "*Lord, what should I do? I am afraid to go in!*" She took a deep breath and gathered her courage, then walked to the door of their apartment.

Inside, she found Frank standing in the front window. She stood quietly, waiting to see what he would do. He turned to her and said, "Cora, where have you been? Why were you outside the door?" She said nervously, "I went to church. I wanted to go, and I didn't have a way to call you, so I went."

Frank said, "Remember my rules? Was I walking beside you? Then why were you outside the door, Cora?"

Cora didn't answer him. She walked toward the bedroom, and he followed her, raising his voice. "Answer me when I ask you a question!" He grabbed her arm, and she said angrily, "Get your hands off of me!" Frank looked at her in shock, then told her to take off her coat because he was going to teach her a lesson.

She continued to the bedroom. Once inside, she started to cry. Falling to her knees, she prayed…

"The Lord is my shepherd; I shall not want.
He maketh me to lie down in green pastures:
he leadeth me beside the still waters.
He restoreth my soul: he leadeth me in the
paths of righteousness for his name's sake.
Yea, though I walk through the valley of the
shadow of death, I will fear no evil: for thou
art with me; thy rod and thy staff they
comfort me. Thou preparest a table before me in the
presence of mine enemies: thou anointest
my head with oil; my cup runneth over.
Surely goodness and mercy shall follow me
all the days of my life: and I will dwell in the
house of the Lord forever."
(Psalm 23 KJV)

She asked God to take her out of her situation, and He gave her **Exodus 14:14**… *"The Lord shall fight for you and ye shall hold your peace." (KJV)*

She sat down on the side of the bed, and Frank walked in carrying a rod. She jumped up and grabbed her coat, then tried to run past him out the door. He hit her on the back, and she stopped and turned around. She said angrily, "Don't you ever put your hands on me again. I'm leaving."

CHAPTER 3

*F*rank saw courage in her eyes—something he had never seen before. She turned around and started toward the door, quoting **Isaiah 54:17**, *"No weapon that is formed against thee shall prosper, and every tongue that shall rise against thee in judgement thou shall condemn." **(KJV)***

She looked at Frank and said, "Nothing you try to do affects me anymore. Keep your hands off me before God puts His hands on you."

He stepped back and told her to take her coat off so that they could talk. She said that she didn't want to talk today, and she would be back later. He yelled, "Where are you going?" She started out the door and said, "I'm going out there to live my life—the life that the devil stole from me. You have a good life, Frank. I don't care what you try to do to me because God is with me, and I am living for Him."

> *"No man taketh it from me,*
> *but I lay it down of myself.*
> *I have power to lay it down,*
> *and I have power to take it again.*
> *This commandment have I received of my Father."*
> ***(John 10:18 KJV)***

Frank said, "Cora! Please don't leave me! Take off your coat and stay so we can talk." Cora shook her head and snapped, "Leave me alone!" Frank moved to block the front door and told her angrily that she was going to sit down so that they could talk. She responded, "No! You can talk to yourself because I am leaving!"

Frank grabbed her coat and tried to pull it off her, and she fought back. He started punching and kicking her, then threw her to the floor. She was crying and calling out, "Lord! Please help me!" She tried to get up and realized she could not move her left arm. Frank picked her up and started choking her, and she looked into his eyes and gasped that she could not breathe.

For an instant, Frank remembered who she was and that he loved her—but the devil whispered in his ear and told him to "teach her a lesson so that she would follow the rules." He picked her up and threw her across the room. She landed on the glass coffee table, which shattered underneath her. One of the chrome legs pierced her head and stayed there. Frank yelled, "Get up!" and then realized that she was not moving.

Racing to Cora, Frank saw the leg from the table sticking out of her head and began to cry, saying, "Oh my God! Oh my God! What have I done? Cora, get up! Get up, baby, please! Let me help you…Cora, please don't leave me! Baby, I am so sorry. I just lost it. I didn't mean to hurt you."

As he knelt next to Cora, begging her to wake up, Frank heard a voice say, "Go across the street to get some help." Frank, sobbing, said, "No! I am not leaving you! What have I done?" Frank again heard a voice say, "Go across the street and get some help." Frank leaned over and kissed Cora's forehead, then said, "I love you."

Frank called for an ambulance, then ran to his neighbor David's apartment. David heard him yelling and opened the door to find him on his knees, sobbing. He helped him up and said, "What's wrong? What is going on?" Frank gasped, "I think I hurt Cora!" He told David that she was in their apartment and begged him to help her.

As David left his apartment building, he saw the ambulance pulling up and yelled for the paramedics to follow him. He opened the door and saw Cora lying on the floor. She was bleeding from her eyes and ears, and her face was swollen and bruised.

The paramedics asked David to step out into the hall; and just as he did, a police officer came up the stairs. He told David they had gotten a call about a disturbance and asked if he knew what was going on. David explained that he was friends with Frank and Cora and that Frank had begged him to come check on her after they had gotten into an argument. The officer asked David if he knew where Frank was, and he said that he did not. He gave the police his telephone number in case there were more questions, then walked away.

When David returned to his apartment, Frank was sitting on the couch, crying. He said quietly, "Frank, what have you done?" Frank said hysterically, "I don't know! I don't know! I just lost my head. Please go to the hospital and check on her!" David agreed to go and said that he would talk to Cora's family, then told Frank that he wanted him to leave because the police would be looking for him, and he didn't want them to find him in his apartment.

As David went to leave, he turned and said, "I just have one question. How could you beat Cora like that? I didn't even recognize her. Frank, she had blood coming from her eyes and ears. How could you do that?" Frank didn't answer him, but instead began to beg David not to put him out. David lost his temper and yelled, "No! Get out! We're not even friends. I'm Cora's friend!" Frank whimpered that Cora had told him to come and David, believing Frank's lie, said wearily, "She is always trying to protect you and make excuses for your behavior. Okay, Frank. You may stay here until I get back." Frank bowed his head and thanked him, and David said, "Don't thank me. I am doing this for her, not for you."

CHAPTER 4

When David arrived at the hospital, Cora's family was there. Her father, Stefon, approached him and asked if he knew what had happened. David said, "I don't. Frank came to my apartment and said he had hurt Cora. He asked me to go check on her because he didn't think she would want to see him." Stefon stared at him for a moment, then said quietly, "Cora didn't make it." David looked stunned. Stefon asked him where Frank was, and he told him that he was at his apartment, waiting to hear how Cora was doing. Her father told him that they should talk to the police before he gave Frank any news.

David followed Cora's father over to talk to the officer that was waiting outside her room. He explained everything, and the officer asked if Frank was still at his apartment. David nodded and the officer said, "Call him and put him on speaker." David dialed the phone and when Frank answered he said, "Frank, are you still at my apartment?" Frank said that he was and asked David if he had been able to see Cora. David said that he had not because the police were in her room. Frank said, "Is there any news? How is she?" David ignored him and told him that he had to go and that he was on his way home.

The officers said they would follow him home and once he ascertained that Frank was still at his apartment, he should text them. They would wait outside until they heard from him. David went up to his apartment…and found that Frank had fled, leaving his phone on the counter.

The police began to go door-to-door, asking if anyone had seen him. When they got to Ms. Sonia's door, she looked at the photo they showed her, then said she had not seen him. She closed the door and turned to face Frank, who was standing in her apartment. "Frank. What have you done?" He responded angrily, "Nothing. Cora and I got into an argument, and I told her I wanted a divorce. She attacked me, and when I pushed her away, she fell and hit her head."

Sonia said, "How badly is she hurt? The police wouldn't be looking for you if it was nothing." Frank said he didn't know, and he couldn't go to the hospital because Cora didn't want to see him. Sonia then asked Frank if he had told Cora about her, and he said he had not told anyone. He asked her to go to his apartment and get his clothes so they could leave.

Sonia refused. She told Frank the police would be watching his apartment. She said she was going to go to the hospital, and see if she could get some news about Cora, who had been her best friend before Frank came along.

Frank agreed and kissed her. He said, "I love you so much, and I want to spend the rest of my life with you." Sonia said, "I love you too, but I feel terrible about what we have done to Cora. For so many years, she sat in that apartment, waiting for you to come home from your business trips…and the whole time, you were right across the street in my bed, making jokes about her. I am just praying she is alright."

When Sonia arrived at the hospital, she saw Cora's sister standing outside. She ran to her and asked how Cora was doing, and her sister said, "She did not make it. Frank killed her." Sonia screamed, "Oh my God! Oh my God! Cora is gone!" She ran back to her car and headed home. When she got there, she opened the door and started yelling at Frank, "Cora is dead! You killed her!"

Frank said, "No I didn't! She hit her head! Come on, Sonia. We have to get out of here." Sonia screamed, "I'm not going anywhere with you! Why did you kill her, Frank? Get out of my house!"

Frank sighed and asked if he could wait and leave that night, and Sonia agreed. After he fell asleep, she called the police and told them where to find him and what time he would be leaving. She felt like turning him in would make things right between her and Cora. As he left the building that night, the police surrounded him and arrested him for Cora's murder.

EPILOGUE

As Frank sat in the courtroom, he was shocked to hear that Cora's cause of death was strangulation and a broken neck. When he heard this, he yelled, "No! That's impossible! She was still alive when she hit her head on the table." His lawyer confirmed that her neck was broken, and he continued yelling, "That is not true. When I threw her across the room, she was still alive!" His lawyer told him sternly to be quiet.

When Cora told Frank she could not breathe, those were the last words she spoke before the Lord took her home. Frank broke her neck while he was choking her, and when he threw her across the room, she was already gone. He was confused as he listened to the autopsy report because he was sure that he had heard her speaking to him.

Cora was not talking to Frank—he imagined it. Cora had always tried to protect Frank by hiding the abuse, and he would always apologize. But this time he had gone too far, and he no longer had Cora to hide his behavior. Frank sat in the courtroom, realizing that he now had to face the consequences of the pain and trauma he had put Cora through.

What you can learn from this story...

You must love yourself and understand that you do not have to put up with abuse. God does not require us to accept abuse in our marriage or relationship. Cora should have separated from Frank and sought counseling for their marriage.

After attending church, Cora was given a way out. Betty offered to help her and provided a safe place for her to stay; but Cora turned down the opportunity, thinking she had to stay in her marriage when she didn't.

God will provide a way out, but *we have to be willing to take it.*

> *"Husbands, love your wives,*
> *and be not bitter against them."*
> **(Colossians 3:19 KJV)**

REFLECTION SECTION

(Share your thoughts here.)

CINDY AND GEORGE

CHAPTER 1

*"He trusts in the Lord," they say, "let the Lord rescue
him. Let him deliver him, since he delights in him."*
(Psalm 22:8 NIV)

George sat quietly in his study, reading his Bible and thinking about his life. He thought about his wife, Cindy, and their ten-year-old son, Michael. He thought about how he went to work every day, took his family to church on Sundays, and went to Bible study on Wednesdays. His family depended on him to keep everything together, and he knew it.

As he was sitting there thinking, he heard the Lord tell him very clearly not to drive to work but to take the train instead. Even though he had just bought a new Mercedes-Benz and was excited to drive it, he was willing to listen to the Lord...so he took the bus to the train station that morning.

On the train, George suddenly felt very anxious. He called Cindy and asked her if everything was okay. She said it was, and he asked her to please take Michael to school instead of letting him ride the bus. She asked him what was going on, and he said he just had a feeling that Michael shouldn't be on the bus that day. After he hung up, he heard the Lord say, "Trust me," and he said quietly, "I do."

As soon as he clocked in, his boss, Mr. Chester, told him the district manager was there and wanted to see him in the office. George hesitated at the office door, and Mr. Emmanuel, the district manager, invited him in and asked him to sit down.

Mr. Emmanuel explained that the area that George worked in was being shut down temporarily, and the employees were being laid off. George said, "What happened?" Mr. Emmanuel said the parts that were being produced in that area were defective, and an investigation was being launched into the reason why. The area would be closed until further notice.

George stared quietly at the layoff notice in his hand. He had been with the company for thirty years. He had never been late and never missed a day of work…and he was the first one to be laid off. He looked up and said, "Everyone on my team is still working. I don't understand—am I the only one being let go?" Mr. Emmanuel said, "They know this is their last day. They are working out their shift, and you are welcome to do the same."

George declined, and Mr. Emmanuel said he would pay him for the day, and his severance package would include six months of salary and benefits. He thanked him and stood up to leave, then turned and said, "Did you fight for us? You are the union rep—did you fight this?" Mr. Emmanuel looked at him and shook his head. "I tried, George, but there was nothing I could do. All six of you are being laid off. I'm sorry. I am hoping once the investigation is concluded, they will reopen and call you back, but I can't make any promises."

As he walked out of the office, George whispered, "I know that God will help me through this. I just have to depend on Him."

George spent the day going from place to place, filling out applications, and praying the Lord would grant him favor. When he arrived home that evening, Cindy and Michael were playing catch in the backyard. He stood quietly and watched them for a long time, thanking the Lord for allowing them to enjoy the blessings they had been given. He could not bring himself to tell Cindy what had happened, so he put on a smile and went to join them in the yard.

CHAPTER 2

George left the house every morning at his usual time. He spent his days filling out applications and praying someone would call. He was finally offered a job, but it paid much less than his old one had. After he had accepted the job, he said, "Lord, this is a big difference from my old job." The Lord told him to take the job and be faithful with his money, and He would do the rest.

Several months passed. George's severance pay was coming to an end, and the bills were beginning to pile up. He begged and pleaded with God to open a door that would keep them from losing everything.

Finally, the day came when George knew he had to tell Cindy what had happened. As he sat in the car gathering his courage, the Lord gave him *Matthew 18:20*, *"For where two or three are gathered together in my name, there am I in the midst of them." (KJV)*

George went inside and sat down with Cindy. He told her that he had lost his job seven months before, and they had been living off his severance package and his low-paying job. The severance was running out, and his current job was not enough to pay the bills. He explained that he did not want her to worry, but they needed to come together to pray, and try to figure out a solution.

Cindy said quietly, "George, why didn't you tell me? I could have looked for a job. We talked about this when we decided I would stay home with Michael, and you promised me if you ever needed help, you would tell me."

George apologized and said he had not wanted to worry her but that the bills were now going past due, and they were going to have to figure something out. He suggested pulling Michael out of his private school, but Cindy said defensively, "I am not pulling him out of his school and away from his friends. There has to be another solution."

George snapped, "I don't like it either, but this isn't my fault. And we also need to put this house on the market and try to sell it before it goes into foreclosure." Cindy stared at him, then got up and walked out. At the doorway, she turned and said, "George, you have come up with all of these plans without even talking to me about it. I know what happened wasn't your fault, but we can try to work through this together."

Cindy grabbed her purse and keys and headed out the door. George asked her where she was going, and she said, "I am going to get some help and to try to find a job." George begged her to keep everything between them rather than going to her family, and she said, "I will be back. I will not lose everything just because you want to walk in your pride." He yelled, "This is not pride! I am just waiting on the Lord!" Cindy snapped, "And the Lord is waiting for you to put away all that pride!"

CHAPTER 3

Cindy *went to visit her mother* and told her about their financial situation. Her mother asked if it was okay to call Cindy's brother, Greg, to see if he could help them, and she agreed.

A few days later, Greg came over to visit and offered them money to pay their bills. George thanked him and declined, telling Greg they would be fine.

Cindy overheard him talking to Greg; and after he left, she went to George and told him he should have taken the money. George shook his head and said, "I heard the Lord, and the answer was 'no.' We must stand still and wait on Him." Cindy looked at George and walked outside to call Greg and tell him they needed the money.

The next day, Greg met Cindy at the bank and gave her enough money to pay their bills. He said, "What happened? George said you did not need anything." Cindy replied, "Yes, we do. George has a lot of pride, but I am not going to live in poverty." She told Greg she would pay him back a little at a time, and he said, "No. I will talk to your husband about it."

A few weeks later, Greg called George and told him he had a job offer for him. He asked if he could stop by and George said he would be home that evening.

CHAPTER 4

G eorge opened the door and invited Greg to follow him to the study. He noticed that Greg was carrying a black briefcase and asked him what he had brought. Greg said, "A way for you to make money."

George sat down, and Greg put the briefcase on the desk in front of him. He opened it and stared for a moment, then said quietly, "What is this?" Greg said, "It is exactly what it looks like." George said, "It looks like drugs. I hope you are not suggesting what I think you are!"

George slammed the briefcase shut and stood up. Greg snapped at him to sit back down, and George said frantically, "I'm a man of God! Why are you doing this? Your family is always bragging about you, but you are nothing more than a low-life drug dealer! Get out of my house!"

Greg said calmly, "I can't do that George. You borrowed money from me, and now you must work it off."

George was shaking. He said, "Cindy told me she got the money from you, and you said it was okay to pay it back a little at a time!" Greg said calmly, "I never said that, George. I told her I would talk to you...and I am talking to you."

Greg walked over and looked out the window with his hands in his pockets. "You know, George. We can make a lot of money in these suburbs, driving around in that brand new Mercedes-Benz. Us working together and in that new car? Wow!"

He walked back over to the desk and looked down at George, who was staring at him with a panicked look on his face. "You know people trust you because you are a trustworthy guy. And you've got that nice car…"

George found his voice and yelled, "So you want me to take the blessing that the Lord gave me and use it for Satan's kingdom? I don't think so. I would die before I turn my back on God! I'm telling you for the last time—get out of my house before I call the police."

Greg started to laugh. "I will tell them you were a part of it all along, and you will go down too. They will ask you where you got the money you deposited into your bank account and what will you tell them?" George looked at him and said angrily, "You are sick, Greg. Sick in your mind. Get out of my house!"

Cindy was in the kitchen making dinner. She heard Greg and George arguing and started down the hall to see what was going on. She stopped when she heard George say, "I told you. I will pay you back. But you know I have to take care of Cindy and Michael." Greg said, "Well, right now you are not doing a very good job of taking care of anyone." George hung his head and sat back down.

Greg continued, "This is my house now. I am setting up my business here, and I don't have time to wait—I need my money."

George told him to get out and not come back, and Greg pulled a gun out of his pocket and snapped, "Get up, George. I am done playing around. You are coming with me." George looked at him incredulously. "Are you crazy?" Greg leaned over and whispered, "Get up NOW or my baby sister will find your body on the floor. Let's go, George."

George said, "If that is your plan then do it now because I am not going to do this, and I am not going anywhere with you." Greg raised the gun and pointed it at him, and he closed his eyes. He thought, "This man is crazy. I've got to get him out of my house and away from my family." He opened his eyes and looked at Greg. "Fine. I'll do it."

Greg said, "Now that I have your attention, I have someone I need you to meet. His name is Daniel, and he will train you. As long as you do everything he tells you to do, you'll be fine."

He stopped and looked at George, who was staring blankly at him. "George!" he hissed. "Are you listening?" He grabbed George's arm and said, "Don't mess this up. Just because you are family doesn't mean that I won't kill you."

Greg walked out onto the patio, and George saw Cindy standing in the doorway. He motioned her to stop and whispered, "Please. Just go back to the kitchen. I will explain later." She nodded and backed away, looking frightened.

Chapter 5

O nce *Greg finished his conversation,* George called out to
Cindy and told her they were going to the store and would
be right back. He had texted her and told her to be quiet, so she
didn't respond.

Greg asked George if he wanted to make sure Cindy heard him
before they left, and George said, "If she didn't, she will text me
when she notices I am gone." Greg chuckled as they climbed into
his car.

Greg handed George a blindfold and told him to put it on. They
drove for a while; and when George took it off, they were parked
in front of a warehouse.

It was a big warehouse. It had four levels with people on every
floor. Greg walked around with George to introduce him and told
the employees George would be working with them and to treat
him right. George looked at Greg and smiled nervously.

*Lord, please get me out of this place. Please save these people. Let your
anointing fall on every head, and if they don't turn from their evil
ways, then destroy Satan's kingdom that has been built on your land.*

Greg dropped George off after midnight. Cindy was on the couch in the front room, waiting for him. She jumped up and ran to him sobbing, "I'm so sorry. I'm so sorry. Did they hurt you?"

She told George they needed to call the police immediately. She said, "I didn't because you texted me and told me not to, but now we need to get them involved. And don't worry about Greg being my brother. I don't care if they send him to jail."

George kissed her and told her he needed to take a shower and then they would talk. As he stood and let the water run over him, he broke down and started to cry. He told the Lord that he was frightened, and he did not want to live in fear. As he stood there, he heard the Lord say, "Trust me. I will never leave you. I have work for you to do. There is a young man working in the warehouse. He prays to me every night. Not everyone there is a part of Satan's kingdom. They are slaves and have been bought for a price. Stand up, and get ready because you are going to help free them."

George wrapped a towel around his waist and went into the bedroom. He turned on the radio and told Cindy to keep her voice down. She asked if he thought someone was listening and he said quietly, "I don't know, but we have to be careful."

Cindy said, "I did as you asked and didn't tell anyone—not even my mother." George said, "Good. We don't know who is involved, and we have to assume she might be." Cindy looked at him and said defensively, "My mother doesn't have anything to do with this!" George nodded and said, "I pray not. But I don't know."

He told Cindy where Greg had taken him and what he had seen. She started to cry and said, "This is all my fault. What have I done?" She looked at George and said, "Please don't get involved in that. We will figure something out." He answered, "I don't intend to get involved. I will find a way out with the Lord's help."

He told her that Greg was coming over that evening to set up and begin using the house, and they would have to play along until he figured out what to do.

CHAPTER 6

The next morning, George told Cindy he had a plan. He told her to hide in the closet and record their conversation. He said it was very important that she remain perfectly quiet and not come out until he told her to.

When Greg arrived, Cindy was already in the closet. She recorded everything like he told her to, and when Greg left she ran out and handed her phone to him. She was crying as she said, "I have to help you put my brother away."

She ran to her bedroom and fell to her knees, crying out to God and begging Him to help George find a way out. "I hate this. It's all my fault," she sobbed over and over.

George walked into the bedroom. He looked at her and said, "You talked about how you didn't want to go back to our old life but look what you have done. This happened because you didn't trust the Lord. You took your way and not the Lord's way! And you did not trust me after I told you the Lord said no; you went behind my back and did it anyway."

"Trust in the Lord with all thine heart; and lean not unto thine own understanding. In all thy ways acknowledge him, and he shall direct thy paths."
(Proverbs 3:5-6 KJV)

George walked over to Cindy and putting his hand out, He asked her to pray with him.

"Lord, forgive us for not trusting you," he began. Cindy stepped back, and George looked at her. "What's wrong?" Cindy said, "You warned me and I took the money anyway." George said, "I am the head of my house, and I allowed you to. I could have given it back to him, but I didn't. God will hold me responsible because I am the head of my house."

George sat down on the bed. He took Cindy's hand and asked her to sit on the bed next to him.

He said, "Do you remember a story we studied one Wednesday night in Bible class? We were talking about Ananias and Sapphira *(Acts 5:1-11)* and how they sold their property. With his wife's full knowledge, Ananias kept back part of the money for himself, then brought the rest and put it at the apostles' feet. Peter asked him if that was all that he had received, and he said it was. Then he asked him why he let Satan convince him to lie, not only to Peter but also to God. When Ananias heard that, he fell down and died. When his wife came in, they asked her the same thing and she too fell dead because she knew her husband had kept the money for himself.

I knew you got the money from Greg, but I didn't say anything. I could have told you the Lord told me you took the money because when I called the bank to make arrangements, they told me our mortgage was current.

God told me to have you to give it back, but I didn't because I didn't want to. I must ask forgiveness as well because I did not do what God told me to do. I told myself it would be okay because you were the one receiving the money, and I told the Lord you would not listen to me. I felt that would justify my actions, just like Adam and Eve.

Adam knew God had told him not to eat of the Tree of the Knowledge of Good and Evil, but he told God that Eve gave it to him and that is why they were both kicked out of the Garden of Eden."

George told Cindy he was not going to do what Greg was asking him to, and he knew that Greg would try to kill him. Cindy shook her head and told him she had heard a lot of things about Greg, but she had never heard anything like that. George said, "Yes, he will. He showed me pictures of a guy that had been beaten to death and said if I didn't cooperate, it would be me."

George got his Bible, opened it and read,

> *"Put on the whole armor of God, that ye may be able*
> *to stand against the wiles of the devil."*
> ***(Ephesians 6:11 KJV)***

Cindy said, "Wow. That is what we are fighting against." She kissed George and told him they needed to get some sleep, and they would come up with a plan in the morning. George said that he had something that he had to do first thing, and she said that was fine.

CHAPTER 7

The next morning, George went and bought a gun. As he was filling out the paperwork, the Lord reminded him:

"For we wrestle not against flesh and blood,
but against principalities, against powers,
against the ruler of the darkness of this world,
against spiritual wickedness in high places."
(Ephesians 6:12 KJV)

He went home and told Cindy what he had done. He said, "You know the devil wanted me to fight in the flesh, not in the spirit. But I will let God deal with your brother." Cindy said, "That's right. We are children of God, and we can't act like the world."

Cindy said she was going to go talk to her mother and see if she could talk to Greg for them. George said that was fine, but she was not to talk to Greg herself anymore because he was crazy. He also told Cindy he was pretty sure her mom knew what was going on because Greg was not one to hide things from his mother.

After Cindy left, George called his friend Derrick, who was an officer with the Narcotics Unit. He asked Derrick if they could meet for coffee because he needed a favor.

Derrick, George, and their friend Robert had grown up together. They lived in the same neighborhood and kept each other out of trouble. Even though they were successful adults now, they were still keeping one another out of trouble. Derrick called Robert and told him George needed them, and they were meeting at his restaurant shortly.

When Derrick and George arrived, Robert had already set up a booth in the back for them. George wanted to be able to watch the door in case someone was following him.

As George was walking in, he noticed a car pulling in that had been behind him on the road. Rather than going to sit with Derrick and Robert, he sat down at another table and texted them, explaining what was going on and what Greg was asking of him. He told them Greg had threatened to kill him if he didn't cooperate.

Derrick texted him back and told him to finish his breakfast and go home. He said he would contact him later.

When George arrived home, Greg's car was in the driveway. The car from the diner had followed him all the way home and parked about half a block down the street.

George kissed Cindy and asked Greg if they could talk in the study. Greg asked him if everything was okay, and he said it was and that he had gone out for a bit that morning to clear his head. He told Greg he was willing to do what he asked, but he needed to keep his day job. As he was talking, he was reminded of Abraham and Sarah and how Abraham lied to the king to save his own skin. He silently asked the Lord to forgive him.

Greg said he could keep his day job, and Daniel could pick him up from there. George asked if he could give him two weeks so he could find someone to take over coaching Michael's Little League team, and Greg agreed.

Greg told George he needed to stay away from the warehouse, and George reminded him that he had been blindfolded all the way there and back and he couldn't have found it if he wanted to. Greg just laughed.

Later that evening, George remembered that it had been a big warehouse and texted Derrick. He didn't know the location, but he described the building; and Derrick said he thought he knew where it was.

Derrick asked for Greg's phone number and told George to try and stay away from him. "If he asks you to go anywhere, make up an excuse."

George explained that he had two weeks and then he would be expected to start doing what Greg wanted him to.

Derrick called two days later and said surveillance showed that Greg was always at the same address. He read it to George, who said, "That's my mother-in-law's house."

George gave Derrick Cindy's mother's name, and he asked if Greg lived with her. George explained that Greg had his own home, but he didn't know where it was. Derrick asked him not to say anything to Cindy, since it was her mother and told George they would be keeping an eye on the house.

Over the next couple of weeks, Derrick noticed Cindy's mother was never home. One day, while he was watching the house, he saw one of his fellow officers go inside. His partner saw it as well and asked him why they were watching the house. Derrick said they had received an anonymous tip about a drug operation being run out of the home.

Later that night, he texted George and told him to be careful and not talk to anyone, even Cindy. He asked George if he had a picture of Cindy's mother; and when he received it, he was shocked to find out that he knew her—she worked in the evidence room at the precinct.

CHAPTER 8

George waited several days and grew concerned when he didn't hear from Derrick. He prayed for him every morning that no harm would come to him, and he would be able to bring the operation down.

The day he was supposed to start, George was expecting Greg to call him—but the phone was silent. He waited for over an hour for Daniel to pick him up, but he never showed.

When he arrived home, there was a scrap of paper on the porch. He reached down to pick it up and realized it was a note from Derrick. It said, **"It is finished."** He looked around nervously and noticed that the car that had been parked across the street for the past two weeks was gone.

George went to his study and opened his Bible.

> *"Fret not thyself because of evildoers, neither be thou envious against the workers of iniquity. For they shall soon be cut down like the grass, and wither as the green herb. Trust in the Lord and do good. So shalt thou dwell in the land, and verily thou shalt be fed. Delight thyself also in the lord: and he shall give thee the desires of thine heart. Commit thy way unto the lord: trust also in him; and he shall bring it to pass."*
> **(Psalm 37:1-5 KJV)**

That night, George and Cindy were watching the late-night news and saw a breaking story about a home that had been raided that day. Cindy gasped and said, "That's my mother's house!" As she was getting dressed, she asked George if he had heard from Greg lately. He said he had not.

The news story continued, and George saw the warehouse had been raided as well. He called for Cindy, and they stood and watched for several minutes. Cindy scanned the people handcuffed in front of the warehouse for Greg, but he was not there. She tried to call him and got no answer. George convinced her to wait until the next day, and they would try and contact Greg and her mother.

The next day, George received a text from Derrick asking him to meet on Bell Street at 2:00 p.m. This was a code—the street was not named "Bell," but the school bell at their high school would ring at 2:00 p.m. Derrick asked George to make sure he wasn't followed.

When George arrived, Robert and Derrick were waiting for him. They sat down, and Derrick explained that they had been watching Greg for years but could never pin anything on him. They had finally busted him two weeks ago, and he agreed to testify against his mother in exchange for a plea deal. Greg's brother had been killed many years before, and he knew his mother had done it. He knew that if he didn't testify against her, they would try and pin it on him.

He then explained that Greg and Cindy's mother had disappeared before they could arrest her. George said that it was time to tell Cindy, as he felt like she deserved to know what was going on, and she might be able to help them find her mother. Derrick agreed but asked him not to use his name.

CHAPTER 9

Cindy didn't believe George at first. She asked him if he knew where Greg was, and he explained that he was in federal custody. She asked to see him, and he said he would see what he could do.

Several weeks later, Cindy was finally allowed to see Greg. She demanded answers, and he began telling her about how he had been working with their mother for years. Calvin, their older brother, had been a part of it as well; but when he told his mother he was tired and wanted out, she had him killed.

Greg said that after Calvin was gone, he was next in line. She had made it clear that Cindy was never to know, but he was telling her now because their mother had put a price on his head, and he knew he would die in prison. He also told her to tell George to watch his back because their mother was still out there, and she was angry.

Epilogue

Several weeks later, Cindy got a call from her mother. She texted the number that she was calling from to Derrick, and he told her to keep her on the line as long as she could.

Cindy asked her mother if she knew what Greg was doing, and she said she did not; and when she found out about it, she had left and moved in with a friend. Cindy asked her why she had never said anything, and she ignored her. She told Cindy she was planning to leave the country and would let her know once she was settled. She said she wanted to send Cindy and George money before she left, and Cindy thanked her but said they would not need it, as George had gotten his old job back, and they were doing fine.

Cindy asked her mom if she could pray with her, but she declined. After Cindy hung up, she got a text from Derrick letting her know they had her mother's location. She texted back, "Please don't hurt her."

Four months later, Derrick was able to shut down the entire operation. After everyone had been arrested, he let George know he could go see Greg.

George had some questions about the young man he had seen the day he went to the warehouse. Greg said his name was "Main," and he had been cleared of all charges and placed into the Witness Protection Program.

Greg looked at George and said, "You look different." George smiled and said, "It's all God." Greg told him he and Cindy needed to forget about her family and get on with their lives. As George stood up to leave, Greg said, "Have a good life, George. Take care of my sister."

What you can learn from George...

Life can change in an instant if you are not prepared for it. The only thing you can do is depend on God. George had to depend totally on God to deliver him because he knew that was the only way out of his situation. His wife was afraid of losing everything. She wanted to fix it right away; but sometimes, it's very hard to wait on God. It can be difficult to stand still and not know if you will survive the attack on your life.

We don't always know why we go through things. But God uses His believers to fulfill His plans. George was a faithful believer and could not understand why his life was turning upside down, but God used him to free the young man who was trapped in a bad situation.

In this story, you have seen how the devil can deceive you into believing he is on your side. He will lead you to believe you can have the world if you follow him.

*"After Job had prayed for his friends,
the Lord restored his fortunes and gave him
twice as much as he had before."*
(Job 42:10 NIV)

REFLECTION SECTION
(Share your thoughts here.)

ACKNOWLEDGMENTS

I thank God for always being there when Satan tried to destroy me and my family.

I would like to acknowledge…

My father, **Mr. Joe,** who was a powerful man of God whom I miss so much. He passed on in October of 1995.

My mother, **Mrs. Alberta,** for her love and guidance. She is still working hard for the Lord.

My sons, **Carnardo**, **Carl**, and **Gabriel**, and my daughter, **Ida**… thank you for standing by me through the tough times in my life.

My siblings, **Faye**, **Kim**, **Tee**, and **James**…I love you so much!

My brother, **Joe,** who passed in 2009. I love you and miss you.

My **friends,** who are great men and women of God, for encouraging me to keep going.

I give my God all the praise and honor
which belongs to Him who is
All Mighty and All Powerful.

ABOUT THE AUTHOR

Ivory Johnson was born in Tallahatchie, Mississippi and grew up in Chicago, Illinois. She is one of six children born to Alberta and Joe. Ivory is the mother of four children.

Her first book, *The Life in God*, was released in January of 2016. She designed a pill cutter with a timer in 2015 and has worked as a financial advisor since 1996.

CONTACT THE AUTHOR

If you would like to contact Ivory Johnson, you may do so at:

Godwaitingroom5@yahoo.com